If it is sentimental, it is still the noblest of desires: "A world with kindness/Is where I dream/We will all live/Someday." Deborah K. Miller's new volume includes not only, "A Place To Dream" but also many other poems devoted to the praise of kindness, humane thought and action, and love. In fact, apart from some descants on aging and mortality, *One for the Road* may be read all through as a paean to familial love. These are pages to hug the heart.

—Fred Chappell,
Poet Laureate of North Carolina, 1997-2002.
His recent book is *As If It Were* (LSU Press).

These bright and hearty poems make Deborah Kravitz Miller's *Remnants of Strawberry Blonde* familiar, yet with more shine and bravado. Every syllable settles in real feelings to consume discord and pain. Love lives in the heart of every poem in *One for the Road*.

—Shelby Stephenson,
Poet Laureate of North Carolina, 2015-2018.
His recent book is *Slavery and Freedom on Paul's Hill* (Press 53).

One for the Road

POETRY FOR LIVING

DEBORAH KRAVITZ MILLER
Author of *Remnants of Strawberry Blonde*

© 2020
Published in the United States by Nurturing Faith Inc., Macon GA,
www.nurturingfaith.net.

Library of Congress Cataloging-in-Publication Data is available.

ISBN: 978-1-63528-096-8

All rights reserved. Printed in the United States of America.

Dedication

This book is lovingly dedicated to family and friends who make the world a kind place, speak for those who have no voice, share their lives without expectation of anything in return, treat people with the dignity they deserve, and work for the greater good of humanity. You know who you are.

Acknowledgments

I'd like to acknowledge my friends who encourage, endure, and sometimes edit my poetic inclinations. Thank you, Nancy Martin-Young, Ellen Rose, Sara Anderson, Dorothy Baird, Sarah Edwards, Ann Hart, Rick Harrison, Preston Martin, and Laura Johnson.

Thanks to Jo Taylor, friend and teacher whose classes/workshops (and patience) have made me a better poet and storyteller.

Thanks to Fred Chappell and Shelby Stephenson, who walked alongside this poet's conversations of the heart and understood the journey.

Contents

Introduction 1

The Game 3

Pipe Dreams 6

The Red Tailgate 8

No Parking 10

A Shoeshine Tip 12

What Seems to Be 14

Perfect 17

Overhauled 18

I Remember 20

Windfall 23

Together 25

My Little One 28

Life Lessons 29

Mother's Day 30

Our Moment 31

The Whisper Beneath My Heart 33

Coffee and Cigarettes 35

Hindsight 46

The Kitchen App 37

Outlook 38

Homecoming 40

Laundry 41

Swept Away 42

Church Anniversary 44

Email 50

Every Day 46

Never Alone 52

When & Ever 54

Gatekeeper 56

Hourglass 58

The Past Present 60

Dear Rebecca 61

High Tide 64

Blessed 66

Wonderings 68

Life's Sprawl 71

Love's Memory 73

Knowing 74

Zip Code 28420 76

A Child's View 78

What I Leave You 79

Even Now 81

A Journey 84

The Red Brick 86

House for Sale 90

Just Life 91

Old Jerusalem 92

Fingerprints 93

Chicken Stew 95

I Will Gather 97

Where I Dream 98

Notes 99

Postscript 101

Best friends and neighbors, the Johnston family in 1959 with Deborah. Pictured here are (L-R) Karl Jay, Konnie, Deborah, and Karen.

Introduction

I grew up in Shallotte, a southern coastal North Carolina town. My mother was from Ash, ten miles inland from Shallotte, and my father was from Brooklyn, New York. My parents believed everyone's life is important. Demonstrations of kindness and compassion were their greatest legacy. I viewed the world through my grandparents' eyes, worked in Dad's furniture store, became a part of a faith community, and had great friends who taught me people are responsible for themselves and should contribute to the greater good of others. Childhood memories formed the backdrop of my adult responses to life's challenges and gave me the opportunity to share these lines with you.

My first book, *Remnants of Strawberry Blonde*, was published in 2013. After one poetry reading, a lady greeted me in a forceful tone, saying, "I did not have the kind of parents and grandparents you had." It was momentarily disconcerting. Then, her voice quieted as she added, "But I can be the kind of grandmother you had." She understood exactly what I tried to get across in my poetry. No matter how our lives appear to others, all of us know love and loss. An attitude of gratefulness changes our view of everyday occurrences, and perhaps another person's life.

One for the Road reveals life lessons through the lens of youth and the perspective of adulthood. Poems span idyllic childhood summer days to the ravages of old age. You'll find laughter, tears, and most of all gratitude for the gift of life and love, the support of family and friends. It is a book best shared with others. These words and your own can create a better understanding of relationships among people. With that, I hope those who follow in our footsteps lead lives acknowledging the dignity and worth of each individual and live life compassionately.

A poem that calls to our hearts can remind us of a wonderful meal shared together before departing to our next destination. We are forever on a journey; memories coalesce moments our lives touch each other. Perhaps it is that first hello, the experience of empathy, a photograph with friends, a goodbye wave, a favorite verse that sustains our spirits over the years. That is the coming and going, the *one for the road,* that counts the most. Safe travels.

The Game

When fireflies light the air,
Shadows brush against the ground,
Leaves swish with a breeze,
The pitcher's on the mound,

You can hear the sound of baseballs
Flying through a starlit night
As the batter hits his target
Over right field, out of sight.

The crowd leaps to their feet;
People clap, shake hands.
It's a homerun celebration
For fans in the stands.

He's the hometown hero
Everyone came to see.
He's the boy down the street;
His heart belongs to me.

To the team he's a number,
Like the miles he walks to school.
To the teachers he's a wonder,
'Cause he's never lost his cool.

Always does his homework,
Says it seems the thing to do.
If you want to go to college,
Better keep up with the news.

You never know who's watching
When you saunter down the halls,
Could be a pro recruiter
Asking you to sign a ball.

He's the hometown hero
Everyone came to see.
He's the boy down the street;
His heart belongs to me.

He was called up to the big leagues,
Got a contract, set for life;
Played the Yankees and the Dodgers,
A different ballpark every night.

No matter where he goes,
No matter where he's been,
When he steps up to the plate,
All the dreams begin again.

He can feel the sudden crack
Of the bat against the ball,
Bases that were loaded
Clear like leaves at autumn's call.

He's the hometown hero
Everyone came to see.
He's the boy down the street;
His heart belongs to me.

One day, crowds will be sparser.
His grip clasps the bat,
In the struggle for denial,
This season is his last.

Still, people flock to see him;
He's the legend of his town.
Friends he knew as children
Greet him here, from miles around.

For a moment, all's forgiven.
He left them back in time.
They're so happy he's returning,
Singing with them *Auld Lang Syne.*

He's the hometown hero
Everyone came to see.
He's the boy down the street;
His heart belongs to me.

Pipe Dreams

Children played in concrete pipe tiling
Below street level where
Water flowed from farms above
Wandered toward Shallotte River.

We were unconcerned about
Germs in a rushing stream,
Only tiny minnows caught
In dime-store goldfish nets.

Bullfrogs croaked and jumped
Through our fingers
Faster than kite string
Spooled out on windy days.

Cool clay beneath our feet
Relieved hot, rainy summertime
Renditions of *We Shall Not Be Moved*
To the neighbor outside the pipe's exit.

Rode bikes through her yard
Coming home from downtown,
Clipped a few bushes
When she chased us with a rake.

It wasn't ever about her,
Only salt air on our faces
Traveling to mystery and power
A meandering creek held over us.

Inside sand-dusted pipe
We heard cars coming,
Braced ourselves,
Believed we helped hold up the road.

Thought we were invincible.
Saw life's shapes flow by in miniature forms,
Rounded rocks perfect for hopscotch
And *ooey gooey* untouchables.

Joyous giggles echoed underground.
Perhaps the tunnel was happy
With children for company
In an open-ended hideaway.

Like clouds skirting a thunderstorm
After rain passes,
Our short-lived time inside the tile
Served us well.

Learned life always swirls,
Moves in unexpected ways,
Those things we hold precious,
And forgotten pipe dreams.

The Red Tailgate

Swinging our legs off a red tailgate,
So excited we couldn't wait
As an old Ford rumbled down a soft dirt road,
Where the best briarberries found did grow.

Thorns scratched our hands when we reached in.
Berries tasted so good we did it again.
Soon our mouths were full, buckets were too.
Our fingers stained a purplish hue.

There's nothing better in this old world
For a country boy and a country girl
Who climbed out the window in the middle of night,
Looked at stars in pale moonlight,
Ran in the grass, lay on sod,
Felt we were held in the hands of God.
There's nothing better in this old world
For a country boy and girl.

Built our teepees in the woods,
Climbed up trees because we could,
Walked down the street to Buster Brown's,
Took the curvy road downtown.

Laughed and joked on our way home,
Two peas in a pod who were never alone.
Though we each lived across the street,
In the middle of the road our hearts would meet.

There's nothing better in this old world
For a country boy and a country girl
Who climbed out the window in the middle of night,
Looked at stars in pale moonlight,

Ran in the grass, lay on sod,
Felt we were held in the hands of God.
There's nothing better in this old world
For a country boy and girl.

Sixty years flew by; I've grown old.
Buried deep within my soul
Is the joy I felt when we first met,
Our childhood lived with no regrets.

I wish you could be here now.
Through the streetlight's glow, somehow,
Our memories live within these lines,
Linked together for all time.

There's nothing better in this old world
For a country boy and a country girl
Than to climb out a window in the middle of night,
Look at stars in pale moonlight.
Run in the grass, lay on sod,
Feel you're held in the hands of God.
There's nothing better in this old world
For a country boy and girl.

We were swinging our legs off a red tailgate…

No Parking

A little child, I prayed a lot
In Mom and Dad's first home.
Five little rooms were
My entire world.

Six years of age,
Several acres of space,
A new house
Where many people visited
Became my new boundary.

I prayed for all who came
Within our doors,
Then went to school,
Discovered responsibility
Beyond property lines.

Led me to seek term limits
On nighttime musings,
Having exceeded my capacity
To deal with humanity
Before bedtime.

Life became a prayer,
Reverence an attitude.
A realization there was
No place for complacency
When a world needs you.

I liked sounds of groceries
Being packaged up and
On their way
To elderly folks
Outside of town.

Prayer is
The movement of one hand
Feeding a person
Unable to feed himself.
One person cannot do it all

But can do something.
There's no time to stop
On life's highway
When prayer becomes
An action verb.

A Shoeshine Tip

A man stopped by, sat right down like he'd been there before,
On the wooden chair, still and straight, outside a furniture store.
How much, he asked, *does it cost to shine this pair of boots?*
Twenty-five cents, was my reply, *in any color you choose.*

He'd seen the posted sign on the storefront glass.
Seeing the boots he wore, I knew why he asked.
Scuffed, torn in places halfway up his calf,
The worst shoeshine job I would ever have.

I sat down, went to work—the brown wax tin was whining;
I used all the paste, made those boots leave shining.
I took my time. I waxed and waned while those old things were drying.
Shined and waxed the wax again, it was almost death-defying

To see them take a sheen—a pleasure for my eyes.
He said in a mocking tone, much to my surprise,
I've seen you shining shoes out here, working on Saturday.
Why aren't you at home, going out to play?

I didn't care to shine these boots, takes up too much time.
After a few minutes work, thought you would resign
Yourself; you didn't give up and quit!
I stopped to have some fun, and you spoiled it.

Sir, I said, *you saw the sign about what I promised to do:*
Shine your boots for twenty-five cents, ten cents for your shoes.
My dad works here every day, sometimes late at night.
This way I get to see him; he keeps me in his sight.

I earn my own money to pay for toys and ice cream.
I make enough on Saturday to pay for anything
My best friends want—even marbles or modeling clay—
And only have to work four hours on one day!

He shook his head, pulled money out from his jacket
    pocket.
I was too excited and nearly dropped it.
The moral of the story is *never be unkind;*
Live up to the words on your advertising sign.

What Seems to Be

Mary Alice Lloyd sat behind me,
Sharpened her pencil extra sharp one day,
Stabbed me through my blouse and pants
A half-dozen times or more and hid giggles behind my back

Not the type of child who caused trouble,
I moved my desk, wished distance
Might distract her attention
Not a chance

Our teacher, Mrs. Smith, needed time
Undisturbed, after our lunch,
So Betty Roach, a high school senior,
Sat silently in her chair

Stoic expression listing across her face
Hand, pencil, and pad waited
For the perfect time
To write our name if we
Spoke or turned around

We'd be paddled, no exceptions,
Excuses, pleas, defenses,
Pardons, vindication,
Forgiveness

Mary Alice realized she hurt me
Slid her chair up, reached around
Jabbed her pencil lead in my left thigh, time and time again,
Until the tip broke off in my skin and I turned around and
    told her, *Stop it!*

Betty Roach spoke up, *I heard you talking;*
Your name's going on the list.
Mrs. Smith returned, looked on the notepad,
Called us one by one to be paddled

My face blood-red
I walked to the front of our room
She said, *I've never had to paddle you before.*
It didn't stop her then

Arrived home and told my mother
I would not go back to school
She looked at holes in my blouse, pants,
Pencil marks on my back, legs,
Pencil tip stuck in my thigh

Called the principal's office
We'd meet him in the morning
Told mom there was no use in going
I went

After all, she was my mother
Brought yesterday's clothes with me
Spoke to the principal myself
Explained what happened

Left alone in his office
In minutes, my teacher appeared
Asked why I didn't speak up
Reminded her, there was *no talking*

I'd never given her any trouble
She was surprised to see my name
On the list—*really*
It shocked me too

Mrs. Smith was a wonderful teacher
I had loved being in her class
But wouldn't go back
I hoped she understood

She spoke to me at eye level
Apologized for the misunderstanding
Both of us with pained expressions
Circumstances are not always what they seem

It seemed to me

Perfect

Tell yourself you're perfectly fine,
With too much to do in too little time.
Grass grows taller than the week before;
Pushing a mower takes ten minutes more.

Get a dog to enliven your way.
You need to find an extra hour a day,
Someone else to prepare for and clean up after
Whose bark echoes sounds of laughter.

Travel to Washington, take your son to chemo.
Hurry back home to a hematocrit that's too low.
A valve repair here, a stent over there,
The body's a fabric, like wash and wear.

Write a poem, giving sway
To incongruities heavily weighed
By lives filled with imperfections,
No time to read recommended directions.

Say *Goodnight* with kindness and grace
In a world pulled apart by money and race.
Love is a Renoir for the ages.
Life, like poetry, is complicated.

Overhauled

He rumbled down the road, an old Rambler.
Face lined with retread tire tracks,
Back swayed from a seat reclining too many times,
Memories dangled from a rearview mirror.

A Cadillac sped down the street.
Flared fins on a '58 glistened in the sun.
Her driver's windblown hair brushed back like airplane
 wings
Kicked him sideways to the curb.

Dusted off his surprise,
Stood in a speedster's shadow,
Poised himself as a Corvette imposter
Of hot rocky nights and fast-action days.

She took him in under her power steering.
Melted into him, molded together on the driver's side.
Vents spewed hot air and smoothed out wrinkles at 70 mph.
They imitated gazelles in a hunter's chase.

Somewhere along a lonesome highway,
Faded dreams dissolved into sounds
Of a 365-cubic-inch engine roar
And scratches across leather seats.

The jolt of spark plugs and
Pistons pumping up and down
Turned the crankshaft of their dreams
Toward a new destination.

No more stares in a showroom window.
New tags and taxes paid,
They split from that place.
His foot pushed the accelerator; her hand turned the wheel.

I Remember

Early 1969 in Red Springs
An ice storm
Snagged power lines.
Girls at Vardell Hall
Left in darkness
Ate melting ice cream,
Sat in candle-lit hallways.

Trees
Dressed in somber silence and
Iced tuxedoes
Rehearsed their next entrance
On Earth's stage
Before an inevitable
Open curtain of sparkling sunlight.

A few days would pass
Before power could be restored.
My father sent you
To bring me
Back home
An unexpected vacation.
I rejoiced.

You were
Thoughtful, kind,
Easy on the eyes
With broad shoulders,
Confident smile,
Heart
I desired.

Entered lobby doors,
Took my suitcase,
Walked me to the car
Like we had done this
A thousand times before
This day
Ever mattered.

Those who wondered
What kind of man
I would choose
Were not disappointed,
Especially the girls peering out
Upstairs lounge windows
On the third floor.

You paid no attention
To their catcalls.
I wanted to turn around,
Tell them
You were the definition
Of *eye-candy*,
And wink.

Halfway home,
Heart racing
At a pause in the conversation,
I asked
What you might think
If I said
I loved you?

Your hands froze
On the steering wheel,
Said I could not love
Someone five years older,
A chilled tone in your voice,
No one would ever guess
You were concerned.

I married a man who brought me
Far more joy
Than tears shed that day.
Still, I never regretted
The experience of loving someone
Even when I discovered a
Heart's desire can be ice cold.

Please see Notes, p. 99.

Windfall

If I were a lightning bug and you were my best friend,
We'd spend summer starlit nights listening to wind
Travel through forests as chimes softly ring,
Sounds move ever closer, rest beneath our wings.
Skyward, touching clouds, our voices soft and low,
We see how, at a distance, time begins to slow.

People walk back and forth; car lights brightly gleam
In circles or straightaways; everyone seems
To never stop, take a pause, share with those they love
Wonders of earth below or skies above.
Each one plays a part in this orbicular life,
Like a line, tail, or frame in spirals of a kite.

We take a self-steered course, navigate and guide
Our lives to distant shores, maneuver them inside
A port of hopes and dreams, wait to be fulfilled
Because of new ideas we desire to build.
Take a closer look, view pathways I've flown,
Flightpaths of friendships, both young and grown.

Measures divided in different beats, they are part
Of many colors in the palette of my heart.
Ocean blue to sunset red, emerald green to white,
All in their own way are creation's delight.
It matters not their station or paths untrod,
We all begin and return to the sod

Where roots grow, branches upward sprout.
In spring all rejoice when leaves blossom out,
Notice subtle changes, warmth in morning sun;
Nature softly rearranges textures of each one.
Her children's lives in woodland, seed to plant to birth,
Genesis to exodus, the cycle of our Earth.

You may find yourself blooming in a crystal vase,
Part of an oak credenza in some executive space.
Along forest floors, with creatures great and small,
Your leaves may be a cover that protects them all.
So let's dream our destiny as we sail around life's bends.
I will be a lightning bug, and you'll be my best friend.

Together

We saw love's first blossom
Cradled softly in our arms,
Our hopes and dreams
For many years to come,
Never an embrace so tender
Or joy more present.

How could we ever
Let them go and leave this place
Called home?
How could the force of love
Separate us from all we
Have ever known?

Decades later,
Meeting by chance,
Love blossomed again
Between us
Like sun rays
Sparkling in morning dew.

Once more we danced
Around the room,
Held fast to new lives,
Claimed promises,
Tender mercies
From younger days.

Springs and summers past,
Orbits around the sun
Remind us
We are older now,

In each other's eyes,
Unchanged.

We will not walk
This way again,
Still desire
Sweet moments
Long-cherished
Years ago.

I lay you down with
A gentle prayer.
You and I held
Children and grandchildren.
We were the fabric
Of all they knew

Kept us close
Until they no longer needed
Their baby blankets.
Who could imagine
Cotton and knitted threads
Had such power over us?

You are imbued with all the love
My heart has ever known.
Remember me as you
Comfort each new little one.
Whisper words of kindness
And generosity.

Surround them with the joy
Of life as you did their parents.
Let them feel the warm embrace
Of generations before them, and
In their hearts
We will live forever.

My Little One

Oh, my little one,
Held you in my arms,
Guarded your safety with my life,
Rocked away your childhood fears,
Smoothed away tiny tears.
You knew I loved you all those years,
My little one.

Oh, my little one,
Your first day at school,
Bright eyes and leather shoes shine.
It's a new ship; you will learn
Facts of life from stem to stern
While the world around you turns,
My little one.

Oh, my little one,
On the road to freedom,
Graduation days soon behind you,
Sweetest dreams are yet to come.
As you share your life with another one,
Together greet the morning sun,
My little one.

Oh, my little one,
Yesterday I held you.
Now I hold on to memories.
I think about you on your way.
In my heart you'll always stay
The way I saw you yesterday,
My little one

Life Lessons

I sit in my rocking chair with you on my lap.
In a few years there'll be no afternoon nap.
Sandcastles and water puddles will call you away.
I'll hear, *Grandma, I'm going out to play.*

Soon you'll be in school, finding a seat on the bus.
Don't be afraid when everyone doesn't look like us.
The world is a big place we all need to share.
People have the same dreams, breathe the same air.

Try to live a life full of kindness and grace.
Keep a smile on your lips a bad day can't replace.
Be the best friend you'd like someone else to be.
Find a faith that sustains you through eternity.

Let hours fill with possibilities, not doubt.
Share life with someone you can't live without.
Remember parents who loved you before birth.
Stay a part of their life while they're on this earth.

Have a respite for the weary, wherever you call home;
Welcome a traveler who has no family of his own.
Know when you give, two people learn to share;
In that circumstance, we're all taught to care.

Life passes by; years flash in minutes.
I look back, remember scenes acted in it.
I can hardly believe all the people I've known,
The work of my heart, my children are grown.

You, with sleepy eyes, head next to my heart,
Make this world better, for another's start.
I'll cherish these *little* moments all of my days.
My love will surround you, now and always.

Mother's Day

I saw my mother yesterday:

In the fullness of my daughter's heart,
Sparkle in her eyes,
A loving kindness from her touch,
Look of sweet surprise.

Perhaps it was her effort
To help someone in need
With a vision of their future,
A rose among the weeds.

Maybe it is just her style
To remind folks, *You have a voice
In planning your own destiny;
Make sure you make the choice.*

Everything she does with love,
My mother's life fulfilled.
As if somehow in our family
It's genetically instilled.

I hope throughout time's ages,
Our family will be able to say,
*I saw my mother's love
In my child yesterday.*

Our Moment

Sat down beside her on an old church pew,
I'd done this many times before.
Her arm on my shoulder, brought us closer,
The mother I adored said,

This is my moment with God,
Someplace quiet where the world settles down.
On a path angels have trod,
With loved ones so dear, journeys seem clear.
This is my moment with God.

Nights turned to days; decades passed by.
Life's scenes were easy to store:
Kissed my children goodnight, turned out the light
With a prayer of my mother once more:

This is my moment with God,
Someplace quiet where the world settles down.
On a path angels have trod,
With loved ones so dear, journeys seem clear.
This is my moment with God.

The day will come when my life will end.
This world will go on as before.
As children come home, they won't be alone.
There's something they know for sure:

This is my moment with God,
Someplace quiet where the world settles down.
On a path angels have trod,
With loved ones so dear, journeys seem clear.
This is my moment with God.

Wherever you go, wherever you are,
We've all been there before.
Here in this place, with the cup and the plate,
The Trinity stretches to four.

This is my moment with God,
Someplace quiet where the world settles down.
On a path angels have trod,
With loved ones so dear, journeys seem clear.
This is my moment with God.

The Whisper Beneath My Heart

Came in from play at the end of day,
Sat down by my mother's side.
She looked at me, hugged me tenderly,
These words she could not hide:

Little child of mine, you're the bright sunshine.
We're together even when we're apart.
Like sand and the sea, a flower and a bee,
You're the whisper beneath my heart.

Life flew by like a twilight sky.
In a minute it seemed I was grown.
First grade gave way to graduation days.
I was married, buying a home.

Came a daughter, a son, new life had begun,
A season of spring to explore.
I said "I love you" a lot and never forgot
To tell them one thing more:

Little child of mine, you're the bright sunshine.
We're together even when we're apart.
Like sand and the sea, a flower and a bee,
You're the whisper beneath my heart.

My mother's years of laughter and tears,
I treasured every moment we shared.
We traded advice that guided our lives
And each, for the other, was there.

Time marches on, like notes in a song,
Her last measure played, she's at rest.
My children are near, my grandchildren hear
The words I cherish the best:

Little child of mine, you're the bright sunshine.
We're together even when we're apart.
Like sand and the sea, a flower and a bee,
You're the whisper beneath my heart.

Coffee and Cigarettes

The worst habits, coffee and cigarettes,
Rarely did they meet, but yet
Every so often on Saturday morn
When cool fall days barely dawned,

Mom sat beside the kitchen window,
Cigarette in hand, coffee cup below.
For a moment time stopped.
Nothing needed she hadn't got.

No neighbor calling, washer's buzz,
Child protesting *just because*.
She had a moment free to dream,
All by herself, or so it seemed.

I stood in amazement, couldn't believe
Her private moments, once unperceived,
Lost in thought, smoke like prayer
Drifted while I watched her there.

Her days would always coincide
With concerns of others identified.
She fixed suppers, gathered clothes
For folks with needs, always those

Who fared worst, kept close to heart,
Opened each door, gave them a start
At beating poverty, other stumbling blocks.
She knew firsthand, the school of hard knocks.

I saw joy she brought to others,
Was so proud she was my mother.
Still, sometimes *I* want to get
A cup of coffee and a cigarette.

Hindsight

Years ago, whenever she needed a ride,
I picked up my granddaughter, Skye.
She could hardly wait for me to see
Pictures she'd drawn, words she could read.

I always told her it would have to wait.
I couldn't turn around—I had to concentrate,
Watch for cars in other lanes,
Pay attention to stoplights, I explained.

One day I left in too much of a hurry.
It was okay; I shouldn't have worried.
I had juice and crackers in a bag.
She could count out ten; that's what she'd have.

She hopped in her car seat, fastened her belt.
Her juice box and crackers she got for herself.
Riding down the road, in the mirror I viewed,
She had a whole handful of crackers to chew.

Gently, I reminded her, *You can only have ten.*
Her reaction was like sails in the wind.
My precious girl, in a sweet little ode,
Said, *Don't look at me, Grandma; keep your eyes on the road.*

The Kitchen App

Configured to live life
In the heat of a moment,
A nine-inch aluminum skillet,
My parents' first kitchen purchase.

Fifty-four years of scrambled eggs and bacon,
It knew certain kitchen secrets,
Mogen David wine in the refrigerator,
Strawberries hidden in the freezer compartment,
Till Mom dropped it on the floor
After a heart attack.

Life signs grew cold between them.
Left alone in the cabinet,
The skillet languished in silence.
Dreamed I heard anguished screams
A hundred miles away.

Finally, a choice to make:
Mother's mink stole or
Her aluminum skillet?

Happy now, it rests in memories
Of a life well-lived, well-loved, and
Occasionally helps me stir up trouble.

Outlook

He sat by a window, watched wind blow
Shadows across the lawn.
Trees sashay, children play
Before another night dawns.

His children are long grown, far from an old home
That brought him so much joy.
He remembers his daughter, fireflies he caught her,
And her own baby boy.

Walls seem to close in, another evening begins,
Second shift answers his call.
Soon it will be bedtime, he questions the fine line
If he really matters at all.

He reaches in his pocket, takes out her locket.
A paper slip falls to the floor.
He reads in surprise, tears fill his eyes,
Know he's loved as before.

We came by for a visit. Our grandkids came with us.
We were happy to be with you.
I know you're lonely. Please know it's only
Two days till we'll be back through.

If you call and there's no answer at all,
Try the same number again.
Put the area code first. Then those other numbers will work.
It'll ring through to us then.

He sits by the window, his face with a soft glow;
Worries are nowhere in sight.
They came through his door, said they loved him once more.
Now he can turn off the light.

Homecoming

Can I go home with you?
The old man asked of me.
I won't take up much room;
I'm good as I can be.

I don't know who you are;
You look like someone dear.
Haven't seen my wife;
She's been gone for years.

Do you know where I am?
I can plainly see
In your eyes I'm here.
Would you stay with me?

Brown eyes turning blue,
In an earlier while
Full of joy and love
For a little child.

My hand cradled his head;
One lay close to his heart.
I'm right beside you, Dad;
We'll never be apart.

He slipped his hand in mine
So softly I could weep.
I said, I'll stay with you
Until you go to sleep.

It is this way in life
From beginning to end.
One hand joins another;
Love ends as it began.

Laundry

T-shirts folded straight from the dryer,
Unlike my eyesight, blurred, wet with tears,
A reminder I will embrace them
On form no more.

Dress shirt, crisp with linen scent,
Neatly pressed into final shape,
A forever note of cotton history,
From a man whose name I shared.

Oh, little one who skipped along
Childhood's road,
Your daddy's girl in distant
Past now comes to lay

Her hand upon life's remnants,
As if somehow I can
Feel the press of
My face against his chest—

His hand gently pat my back,
Brooklyn brogue
Once again assure me
Life will *be okay.*

Washing wheels spin and stop.
Dry cycle unfolds memories
Of another generation,
Promises kept.

Swept Away

I know how it feels to be swept away:

In a mother's arms the day you are born
In a lover's eyes on an autumn morn
By call of sea, surf, and sand
By waving motions of a little child's hand

Through endless ages, among stars of night
Through lingering tastes of a great chef's delight
Within a tear on a wedding day
Within a prayer a child can say

I know how it feels to be swept away:

In instant pain of loss and despair
In realization no one will care
By work of your heart and lines on your face
By passage of time that will all work erase

Through coldest winter with no cover shared
Through heat of summer with no shade of care
Within sounds of a hurried *goodbye*
Within knowledge that all beauty dies

I know how it feels to be swept away:

In moments our memories flash on the screen
By life's end they seem like a dream
Through trial and error we persevere on
Within gentle rivers rhyme is forgone

Into this sojourn we have called life
By the sum of our days and passage of nights
Through flowers in meadows we run with desire
Within us hope our lives will inspire

Those who remain on the playground to play
Now you know how it feels to be swept away

Church Anniversary

Still, we are here.
Thirty years
Young and old and older still,
We, a whisper
In God's heart.
This wandering of Disciples, Baptists, Catholics,
Many others,
Some with faith, some with doubt
Found God in the stillness together.
God must have loved that moment of silence
Before our existence,
Thought of all we could become,
What we could share,
How we would change
Our lives and others.
We look back,
Rejoice in our time together,
Messages of faith and responsibility.
In moments of hardship
We were never alone.
    We knew who we were,
What/who we should be.
We are people of the Table.
We welcome all
As we were welcomed.
In this place, every heart
Returns like a child to a loving home,
Knows he/she belongs to
Someone/something
Greater than this existence.
We are the tears of joy in grief's passing,

Beacon of hope
In seas of despair,
A place of rest
For weary travelers.
We ask for mercy,
Know our hands should show it.
Our words heal,
Our lives reflect
That all of us, whispers in the heart of God,
Are God's promise to each other.
We are Covenant.

> Please see Notes, p. 99.

Email

The email box was full.
A letter from my daughter arrived.
Read the first line of her note,
I sat down and cried. It said,

I know you've grown old.
Words broke my heart in two.
What was she trying to say?
I better read it through.

She said, *I never have much time*
With my job and family.
It's just the way the world works.
You know they depend on me.

But I thought yesterday
About the childhood I had,
How lucky I have been
To have you, Mom and Dad.

I know you miss me coming by.
I miss your warm embrace.
We have to carve out some time
To meet somewhere, someplace.

I wanted you to know
That I love you still.
Don't think 'cause you've grown old,
Love changes, never will.

I sat down to send a reply.
Truth can be abrupt.
I started out by saying,
I know you've grown up, but

I was thinking yesterday
About the childhood you had
And how lucky we have been
To be your mom and dad.

While we enjoy grandkids
And love their embrace,
We have to carve out some time
To meet somewhere, someplace.

We want you to know
Mom and Dad love you still.
Don't think 'cause you've grown up,
Love changes, never will.

It is that way, in our lives—
Words sometimes can't express
The depth of emotion that we feel,
Warmth and tenderness.

Each grateful in our own way
To live the life we've led,
An appreciation for all we have
In life's flowerbed.

*We blossom and we flourish
With nature's loving care.
Growing tall, or short and sprigged,
Air and sun we share.*

*We may feel a winter's chill,
Perhaps a summer's drought.
In the same playing field,
That's what life is about.*

*So as years roll by,
In moments quiet and still,
Don't think 'cause you've grown up,
Love changes, never will.*

Love,
Mom

Every Day

It's Sunday night,
Dinner at home,
Chairs at the table are filled
With voices excitedly
Sharing news
Of dreams being built.
Though everyone's here,
There's still a void
When I think how life used to be.
I want you to know
I haven't forgotten
All you meant to me. And,

I miss you, Mom and Dad.
I miss you every day.
The kids are all fine, grandkids divine,
They often come over to play.
Growing up kind and strong,
Just like you taught me to be.
In their smiling faces
Shines grace of the ages,
Compassion and humility.

Sometimes when the telephone rings,
I think it must be you on the line.
I can't wait to tell you
How well they're doing.
They make me proud all the time.
Everyone works,
Gives back.
Life passes by faster each day.

I look in the mirror,
See your reflection,
And just have to say,

I miss you, Mom and Dad.
I miss you every day.
The kids are all fine, grandkids divine,
They often come over to play.
Growing up kind and strong,
Just like you taught me to be.
In their smiling faces
Shines grace of the ages,
Compassion and humility.

It's a Sunday night
Dinner at home.
Chairs at the table are filled.
Young voices excitedly
Share news
Of future dreams being built.
Our children will see/
Feel love surround them
When we are no longer there.
May our memories live
With those we loved,
In their silent prayers, of

I miss you, Mom and Dad.
I miss you every day.
The kids are all fine, grandkids divine,
They often come over to play.
Growing up kind and strong,

Just like you taught me to be,
In their smiling faces
Shines grace of the ages,
Compassion and humility.

I miss you, Mom and Dad. I miss you every day.

Never Alone

She slipped into my office
Like a light summer breeze,
Asked why death happens to old people.
Death comes to all of us.
We're only here for a little while.
That's why it's important
To love and care for each other.

Quiet for a moment, my six-year-old
Granddaughter burst into tears.
All of my family will die,
Leave me by myself.
I'm the youngest.
I won't have anyone.
You'll be gone.

I held her close.
We will live as long as we can.
You are a wonderful little girl
Who will love many people.
They will love you.
You will never be by yourself.
Don't worry.

She dried her eyes,
Left her playing with stuffed animals,
Walked into my bedroom,
Closed the door,
Sat down on my bed.
Today I had buried my dad.
She had placed a rose upon his casket.

I cried for my loss,
Sorrow in her life
My death will bring.
Hope the memory of love,
Joy of our time together
Is enough to ease the pain
For us both.

When & Ever

What happens when love departs
From the confines of our hearts?
Does it flow like palatial seas
Outward through our galaxy,
Scatter among lightning strikes,
Beam starlight across dark nights,
Murmur hope in evening shadows,
Or healing words when it matters,
Shine through sunrays after rain,
Lay in dust on desert plains?
Love is a simple, noun-ish word
For what should be an active verb.

Love's more than to have and hold.
It moves with us as life unfolds,
Bends with every curve we make,
Forgives us for our mistakes,
Reminds time and time again,
Our being is as it began,
A twinkling in creation's eye.
From chaos came this reply,
Calling forth unending grace
In human form to bravely face
Our place in this universe,
Shows love was present first.

Will we ever understand
Life's gift, which commands
Care for ourselves and others?
One is not without another.
To plow fields, search skies,

Write concertos and lullabies,
In difficult times stand tall,
Welcome strangers, one and all.
This is the synchronicity of souls,
Those who envision and embold
Love's language in every heart
When from the confines, it departs.

Gatekeeper

A dream lay on the forest floor.
    Iron-clad, it would rise no more.
        Greeted night skies like morning rain.

Stuck, as a nail encased in clay,
    A barefoot child walked that way.
        Stumbled o'er the dreamer's last refrain.

She knew within a second's sight,
    This melody drawn from every night,
        Long forgotten in sunlight hours.

Swirled beneath her feet,
    Into her breath it was complete.
        Brought color to fields of flowers.

She pushed on through saplings tall.
    In a clearing she saw them all
        As they waited excitedly for their turn.

Ticketholders held in place,
    Faces filled with years of grace,
        Found exactly what they yearned.

Young and old stood in line.
    Stardust twinkles in Loblolly pines—
        Everyone she had ever known.

Kindred spirits present now,
    As if from this site somehow
        They were finally going home.

Before them one last choice,
    With affirmation in their voice,
        To live in the embrace of heaven's light.

Slowly, the gate lifted clear.
    Goodbyes, simply, *I'll see you dear.*
        Nevermore again to say *Goodnight.*

Walked from one life to another,
    Mothers, fathers, sisters, brothers.
        Her time would have to wait.
Many dreamers still to come,
    There, when her job is done,
        Someone, for her, will raise the gate.

                        Please see Notes, p. 99.

Hourglass

When I am at evening tide
Beneath a child's step toward the sea,
Where lovers shared wedded bliss
And vows through eternity

May I be swept to ocean depths
Feel Earth's power in the might
Of the Mariana Trench, where
Darkness is transfixed by light

Waves deliver me to distant shores,
Caught in a dust devil's swirl
To travel through desert sands
Past kings who ruled this world

Held secrets of the Nile,
Moved into other lands,
Centuries surely fly like
Centurions on their final stand

Made way through jungles steep,
Explored valleys, cold and dark,
Raced to the top of mountain peaks,
Returned to hear morning larks

No samurai or conquistador
Dared make a single move
To obstruct this chosen path
Even if they disapprove

Eons of life's journeys
Culminate in its beginning
As a sandcastle on the shore
A grain of sand has no ending

I'm part of the hourglass of life
As civilizations rise and fall
An inert speck of consciousness
I am my all in all

The Past Present

A long-forgotten gas stove
Thirty inches high
Purchased at a flea market
I take it apart outside
Piece by piece

> Clean rusted burners
> Strip asbestos linings
> Replace door springs
> Paint surfaces
> Polish weathered gas valves
> Reveal a sacred symbol
> Perverted by the Reich
> Ninety-degree angles
> United a country
> Eradicated six million
> Over seven decades ago

Memories burn my cheeks
Restored, the stove sits in
Silent repose
To be turned on
Never again

An ant disappears inside
Just like my grandmother's family
Disappeared in the 1940s.
Sometimes I struggle to keep this relic
I am a Jewish woman with a Nazi gas oven

Dear Rebecca

This is not an apology.
You've no idea how after a reflection of fifty years
I still revel in that glorious moment
At Vardell Hall.

Bound to happen from that first day
Upstairs on 3 East.
We met others who climbed steps,
Found their rooms, moved in.

Said you were just *a farmer's daughter*.
Outside a third-floor window
A big car backed up to the dock.
People struggled to unload a trunk packed with dresses.

You were smart and beautiful,
A quintessential example
Of southern grace
And culture.

We loved you, even if
You were a bit too perfect.
Friendships
Made us all feel safe.

Accidentally realizing your
Fear of things that went
Bump in the night (like us)
A plan was put in place.

With full knowledge of your roommate
Who remains unmentioned,
Suzanne slipped under your bed before
Lights out.

A few minutes later
Muffled sounds,
A thump or two on the mattress,
Your feet hit the floor.

Suzanne reached out,
Grabbed your ankle.
The best blood-curdling scream ever
Erupted from your lips.

We raced down the hall,
Thought you would be relieved
Your ancestor wasn't trying
To reconnect with you.

No, you were mad as *a wet setting hen,*
An accurate southern description
Of your facial expressions and physical movements.
Suzanne rolled around the floor in uncontrollable laughter.

Now you were truly one of us,
Another schoolgirl.
Of course, the hall mom
Called us in for a talk.

It was no help when you
Spoke in your best southern style,
My family has a history of heart trouble.
I could have had a heart attack and died!

It was a possibility.
It didn't happen.
You kept your manners intact.
Your mother would've been proud; we were.

Thanks—you let us in your life
That night and days afterward,
And you forgave us,
Or so we thought.

Mrs. Shooter did her best
To impress upon us
The seriousness
Of what occurred.

If her lips had not inadvertently formed
A smile every now and then,
She might have pulled it off perfectly,
Just like Suzanne.

You were a remarkable young woman and good friend.
Each of us learned life lessons at Vardell Hall.
Authenticity was best—sometimes found
With a healthy dose of laughter.

Please see Notes, p. 99.

High Tide

This calcium carbonate shell
A life form like my own
Navigates ocean currents
As I MapQuest asphalt highways

Our journeys swirl
Around family
Community
Sea swells and inkwells
Course the landscape
Document
Our wanderings
Across the years

Bits and pieces
Are cast aside
Taken by collisions
Of ideas, territory
Self-worth, survival

Touch
Can be pleasurable
Poisonous
Ever-changing
Along the way

Time is friend
And enemy
In a pursuit to ensure
The survival of our families

Though we become
Sand along shorelines
Grains beneath darkest depths
We are the foundation
Of other generations

Forever we remain
Within an ocean's heart
The sky's horizon
Traveling across the universe

Blessed

An antique store, an antique chair,
My grandma should be sitting there
With a smile on her lips, voice calling my name.
The sweet, soft chorus she always sang:

I bless you now as I blessed you then.
Godspeed, my child, may you rise like wind.
Live your life by sand and sea
Until your heart returns to me.

How I long to touch her work-worn face,
Cradle hands that gave me life's embrace,
Taught me love, to be held, must be free
As I heard the words she sang to me,

I bless you now as I blessed you then.
Godspeed, my child, may you rise like wind.
Live your life by sand and sea
Until your heart returns to me.

So in my life, down through my line,
Children and grandchildren from time to time,
As they tell stories of our family tree,
Will repeat this version of history:

I bless you now as I blessed you then.
Godspeed, my child, may you rise like wind.
Live your life by sand and sea
Until your heart returns to me.

I walk outside the storefront door,
A picture framed, I didn't notice before.
The old woman stood by her little white house,
Zinnias and chickens wandering about.

A closer look—how could I not
Remember a face time forgot?
A long-lost memento far away from home
Now returns to cherish a memory owned, and

I bless her now as she blessed me then.
With Godspeed I rose like wind,
Remembered life by sand and sea,
Our hearts together through eternity.

And I bless her now as she blessed me then.

Wonderings

Sometimes
When it rains
Memories of life
Run down my cheeks
Thinking of
Choices I made
Leading to that moment.

Who purchased a house
At an address I never used
Said *hello* to neighbors
I've never known
Selected a career
I never explored?

Married a man
I never loved
Mothered children
I never raised
Found faith
In a church I never visited
Took my place?

Was she kind-hearted
Cared what happened
To an old street person
Loved her family
Talked to her friends
Stood up for what is right
Voted her conscience?

I hope
Her hours were filled
With works and prayers
I've held in my heart
Love, freely given
Received
Transformed.

The day will come
When we meet
At an intersection
In time
Discover our separate
Chosen paths.

Perhaps we'll marvel
At roads traveled
Coming and going
The same moment
Different directions
Living separately
Together.

Find we would have
Made great company
Each for the other
Blessed
In our own way
Became a blessing.

Persevered
Through beautifully
Disguised opportunities
Which looked like
Roadblocks
To the fainthearted
Among us.

If I cannot find her
Maybe she will find me
Because sometimes when it rains
Memories of life
Run down her cheeks
Wondering where I am.

Life's Sprawl

A landscape traversed with
Fortune cookie cutter directions
Hope a pinch here and there
Will tidy paths
Show street signs
Provide an opening where

Sunlight edges souls
Languished under pretense of
Disengagement
To start with breath
Slow, measured,
Fast, unfettered

A before and after repetition
Of all within us
Chance that in a moment
We gift ourselves
Possibilities of reflection,
Forgiveness, new endeavors

Breath is a flutter
Of words in air
A surprised exhalation
Incoming gasp of
New love's arrival
Old love's embrace

We breathe
In the beginning
Of creation's artistry
Humanity discovered

In rhythmic
Simplicity

Passing one to another
This living stream
Moves through
Like a faint ocean breeze
Till some days end
Others begin

A remembrance of
The luminescence
In eternity's shadow
Which prepares us
For the journey with
One lasting breath

Love's Memory

I remember the first time
Everyone does
On some level
Touch evokes
Sensations that
Cascade through every pore
Open to scent
Of skin to skin
Soft and supple, gentle and strong
In the same instant.

Reaching skyward
    I am lifted up
    Arms enfold
All my senses
Eyes reassure we are one together
Despite distance or decades apart
Lips reveal a lifetime story
Ever as tender
Ever as pure
This love.

I live it over and again
    First memories
    My mother lifted me up
Looked into my eyes
I gazed back at her
My cheek gently brushed across her face
Her arms held me close
As once before
When we were one breath, one heartbeat
One embrace.

Knowing

Six weeks ago, he stopped eating chocolate bars,
Little Debbie cakes, chocolate chip cookies,
Peanut butter crackers, and potato chips.
Three weeks ago, he stopped all nourishment.
Two weeks ago, he got up, drank two cans of Pepsi,
Ate a big lunch, went to the front desk,
Talked a while, then back to bed.

We had our last real conversation,
Says he is *just tired*.
I said I loved him and appreciated
All he had done in my life.
Married a wonderful woman,
Gave me a great childhood,
A loving home, a good education.

We scrambled eggs together at breakfast
In a little aluminum frying pan,
Hid frozen strawberries
In back of the freezer from each other.
He painted a hopscotch design on the bottom driveway of
    our home,
Showed me how to be kind and generous with my life.
On Friday nights, we delivered groceries to the *old folks*.

Taught me responsibility,
Explained payables and receivables
When he worked at the furniture store on Saturdays.
His long hours supported our family.
Never gave up when life looked bleak,
Never regretted an unappreciated mitzvah,
Always remembered to tell me he loved me.

When I stopped talking,
He simply said, *Well, I'm satisfied.*
Seemed at peace with himself.
Another week passed; so did he.
A guy with soft brown eyes I adored,
As big a kid as I was little at one time,
A father who made me believe I could be anything

He never told me what I had to become.
He prayed for me to be happy, well, and
Helped me navigate my choices
Oftentimes in several different languages
To make sure he got my attention.
He was a real *character*.
I wish you could have known my father.

Zip Code 28420

On Hwy 130
Traveled to the beach
Pines whispered my name
As I neared Ash, NC
So sweet, soft
A movement of sound
Like the gentle brush of a tear
From my eyes

Grandma's voice calls me
Reminds me where I belong
I see her in fields below
The old homeplace
Supper cooked on a wood stove
Feeding chickens
Everywhere I am
She is there

No one says your name
Like Grandma
Gathers you by her side
Protects you
Makes your favorite meal
Reluctantly lets you go home
Grandma's arms are longer
Than a mother's arms

She embraces generations
Who come after her
Hugs are tighter
Because she realizes
All time in this world
Everyone she has ever loved
Is contained within *hello* and *goodbye*
Moments across eternity's threshold

She watches earnestly
As you grow taller, stronger
In life's seasons
You are a secret garden
Overhanging dreams in her heart
Perhaps your life will
Redeem inequities of past times
With hope for the future

Skies are always blue
Thunderstorms a blur
When she takes your hand
And you walk beside the ocean
Together, the world
Always seems better
When Grandma
Welcomes you home

A Child's View

Walked into my daughter's room,
Feeling sad,
To tell my granddaughter
That stuffed animals I had

Kept for so many years
Now must be put away,
Admittedly unprepared
For what she had to say:

Don't worry, Grandma.
Please don't be sad.
I'll take care of them;
You'll be glad.

When you grow old,
You'll live with me, and then
You can love them all,
All over again.

What I Leave You

You said these hours
Seemed perfect
First-grade friends
Ran along shorelines
Built sandcastles
Found sea glass

Collected shells
Flew kites
Without care or worry
Just sun, sea, sand
People who loved you
And were loved in return

You anticipated each wave
Laughed as everyone
Jumped over and into
Salty rhythms of
Tide's flow in and out
Underneath your feet

Gulls and terns
Zigzagged across skylines
Dived for fish
Scavenged lunch crumbs
Fed themselves
And their young

The beach bustled with
People who fished on the pier
Played volleyball
Laid on beach towels
Caught the sun's rays
Until dusk

Look at you now
Tousled hair and specks of sunburn
Scattered across your shoulders
Wrapped in a blanket
The sea and I have rocked you to sleep
On the cottage deck
You are my blessing
Steps you take
To show kindness and generosity
Those who follow your example
Will be memories of our family's life
Across the centuries

So I gave you
A day like today
A night like tonight
My best wishes and fervent prayer
That my love for you
Will be your legacy to the world

With what I leave you

Deborah (age 4) with Novella Hewett.

Even Now

It's a picture of Novella and me
Taken sixty years ago
A hot summer day
On the side lawn
Of my home
Snuggled close as sisters
Her mom, Videre, left me in her care
For safekeeping

There's no photograph of Videre
So I see her
Every time I look at us
I'm always reminded of
How people treat each other
Alongside my mom
Videre helped our house
Run smoothly

I was almost five years old
Young enough to add years
Not good with division

My skin was white
Hers was brown
Simply the way it was
Didn't know it kept people apart
Until one day

When my best friend and I were playing
We each tried to outdo the other
Comparing toys, marbles, slingshots
Flip-flops and board games
Then he called Videre a name
Neither of us understood what it meant
We knew it was bad
Picked up a tree branch

I hit him time and again
Tore his shirt and skin with every blow
Until he got away from me
Ran to his house, screaming
I went inside, almost breathless
Proud to defend
Someone I loved
Protected Videre, my friend

A victory short-lived
She asked what happened
I told how I beat him
After he called her a bad name
Lost the fight in my explanation
Saw her shock
Her face was downcast
She was so hurt

What had I done
How could I be so cruel
To speak the name he called her
I hadn't understood
I broke her heart
Videre took me in her arms
We cried together
She said it would be *okay*

I knew it was a lie
It would never be *okay* again
Mom arrived back home
Told her what happened
We all wept
Tears never washed away the
Enormity of pain I caused
Now I knew the truth

Words could break or heal spirits of
Anyone or everyone
Including me
I look at Novella and myself
In that picture
Give thanks for my mother and Videre
They loved their daughters
Taught us to love each other

A Journey

Life leaves us in one last breath
Enters the universe, a welcome guest
Its place to take among stars
Till those who loved us from afar

Relinquish their eternal chase
Glimpse creation's warm embrace
Join us, timeless and free
On our way through eternity

It matters not what we owned
Skills and techniques finely honed
It's our spirits and energy
Allowed to soar and finally

Bereft of prejudice and fear
Open hearts and eyes see clear
The story hidden within verses
An ending flame that traverses

This sphere of time, place, intent
Our lives now still represent
We who dwell among the vines
Filled with courage and well-designed

Visions from eons past
Feel wind, climb the mast
On a ship we've yearned to sail
With gusting winds, long-prevailed

And kept hearts alight with hope
Dreams our lips have often spoke
Stanzas lifting spirits high
When darkness fell, we denied

Gloom and despair to take toll
For we are immortal souls
Finding light in a shadow's guise
Till the next beginning of our lives

The Red Brick

It waited over forty years
Underneath the front porch
In line with others
Secure as a supporting actor's first Oscar
Clasped to his heart

Eighteen inches off the ground
Held in a concrete pattern
With others whose shape and size
Made them the right fit
For the foundation of this place

The one brick's deeper red glaze
Stood out with me
Their redheaded granddaughter
Beside blue velvet pansies whose petals
Were in striking contrast

The brick settled there
In the early 1900s
When my grandparents
Built their home
Prepared the foundation

Laid joists
Nailed planks
Framed walls
Raised a roof
Planted flowers

It survived winter's chill
Held up uninsulated walls as
Hurried little feet
Jumped into a
Deep feather mattress

Listened to cries on a Christmas morn
With no Santa sleigh or jingle bells sighted
But finally an apple
Penny candy
To mark the day

Rhode Island red chickens
Followed a trail of corn
Around the brick in the front yard
Where Duroc hogs
Escaped their pen

The brick always appeared straighter
When pictures were made
Family standing front and center
Old people in the middle
Younger ones gathered round

I remember that night
They wouldn't let me
Go to Grandma's house
In the morning they said
She had passed away

No more to see Grandma's face
Or feel her fingers curl my hair
At least one thing remained
In place
One less piece of grief to bear

In a few years
All remembrances
Of my grandparents' full lives
Lived alone in
An empty structure

Heard a rumor
Someone tore the house down
To build a new one
My heart chipped into
A thousand pieces

I imagined
Nails groaned, tin shrieked
When yanked from the roof
Sides of the house crashed
Their broken spines splintered into the ground

The special brick
From my childhood days
All I had ever known
Was swept away in a few hours
Years compressed in a heap of rubble

Later I found my brick
Rested with its family
The backhoe
Failed to destroy everything
Mine for safekeeping

It held recollections of
Struggles and successes
Grandparents, aunts, uncles
Our family dinners
Cousins who played there

The brick, a silent witness to my lineage
A mixture of sand and clay
Viewed the world with me
From a little white house
By the side of the road

Reassured me the measure
Of our lives is less about
The dust of our bones
More about memories
In our hearts

House for Sale

My wrist turns the knob of an old front door
These folks don't realize I lived here before
Recalled memory of my parents' embrace
Childhood joy reappears on my face
There'll never be a place like the one you call *home*

Azaleas brightly flower from sixty years ago
Remembered hours I watched my mother sow
Seeds of compassion rooted deep in ground
Brought calls to action from silence to sound
There'll never be a place like the one you call *home*

I picture this house from an earlier age
Wisdom learned with each turn of a page
From books read by day, dreams by night stars
You'll always be here wherever you are
There'll never be a place like the one you call *home*

You can't go back, they'd like you to believe
Doesn't hold true whenever you retrieve
Life's and love's lessons, sealed within your heart
No one else lived it, and you knew from the start
There'll never be a place like the one you call *home*

Just Life

She's nine
Loves Squeezy Tail
AKA Hippo
A little green hippo
Who arrived on her birth day
Sometimes she thinks Hippo is real
Believes Hippo has a soul just like she does
Hippo sits in one position when she leaves for school
And seems to have moved when she gets home
Says she would like to live forever
If she could stay the way she is now
A child living with her mom and dad
When I become old and die
One of my friends has to put Hippo in my arms
Hippo will also die when I die
This way our memories will be together

Old Jerusalem

In a place I've never been before, I am
home. I wander and wait for the right
moment to walk across my ancestors' cobblestone
roads to an old city market. Faces creased by the
sun's rays and heavy burdens of some days' wear are
too familiar. We come from the same place.
They speak, and my grandparents' voices
whisper inside my heart, *We knew you
would bring us home.* I feel every
grain of sand beneath my feet; travelers'
dust settles on my pants, wind whirls
scents and sounds from centuries ago
around my shoulders. I surrender to a
memory I don't possess. My family's
years of exile flood my senses—
dispersion, settlement, flight of feet,
flight for life, death of dreams and new
family trees, intertwining events
propelling me toward my final
destination. The Wall awaits my
presence. At its face, a lock of
hair from my mother, father, and myself
falls to the ground. Footsteps crush
our DNA into the land. I say a prayer
and place a note in the Wall crevice, which reads,
Mom and Dad, we are finally home.
　　All my love,
　　Your daughter

Fingerprints

Scrubbed those marks a thousand times
Bid them all adieu
Cleaner sprays front door glass
I begin anew

Lately I've reflected
Upon years spent
Wiping away memories
All they represent

Kids rustled to go outside
Wanted to come back in
Drink milk and eat a cookie
Before they played again

Little smudges of chocolate
Thumbprints of creekside clay
Steadily moved upward
As they grew day-to-day

Many times they called me
Waited patiently at the door
Always needed something
They counted on me for

We take this view for granted
Looking inside out
Days remain the same
Years change us, no doubt

Now they've all grown up
Grandkids took their place
Another set of smiles
Time will not erase

Their antics keep me moving
Faces glow in morning sun
A thousand questions answered
By the time evening comes

I'm in no hurry to see them go
Each one part of life
I've lived for them, they for me
As I bid them goodnight

Chicken Stew

Followed Grandma's footsteps like a chickadee,
Rounded the corner of the house,
Face-to-face with an old Rhode Island
Red hen, none too happy to see anyone near her
Nest, and intended no one should take
Another step closer, not Grandma and certainly
Not me.

Grandma wanted to tell me their history.
Someone told her they were sweet
Chickens to raise. That's what she said to me.
Forgot to share that story with the chicken
Who chased me around the yard. I didn't like
To think about chickens killed for food. This one
Swayed my thoughts in another direction.

Even the old rooster appeared intimidated with
The hen's squawks and frenzied rush to get me out
Of her sight. Grandma liked to collect those brown
Eggs daily from her chickens, and she would
Do it today without any help from me. I no longer
Cared about where they came from or how many eggs
They produced.

I didn't know in a year Grandma would be
Laid to rest in the Griffin Cemetery down the road,
Her parents and siblings nearby. Grandpa looked so old
After she passed away. In his younger days I saw him
Dressed up to have a picture made of himself,
His Duroc hogs and his Rhode Island red hens.
That was all forgotten now.

I wrapped my fingers around his hand. Hoped he would
Remember it was still important to get the eggs when
We came to visit. Felt like I needed to be his helper.
Suddenly, I realized there was no noise from the chickens.
That old hen must have made it in the stewpot one day
When I missed being there. Grandpa didn't
Need that aggravation anyway.

I Will Gather

Dust of bones, seaside cliffs
Red clay fields, sediment shifts
Winter streams of snow and ice
Rows of wheat, barley, rice
Summer breezes, October rains
Sunset's majesty across open plains
Pine tree scents, red rose thorns
Birdsong lullabies in early morn
Every sorrow ever sown
All joy we have ever known
Campfires burning throughout night
Stories told to fear's delight
Rustled leaves and wild blackberries
All the kids my arms can carry
Close to my heart, deep in my soul
Everything life can enfold
Dreams of dreams to be fulfilled
All the blessings love instills
I will gather

Where I Dream

People said Grandma's hands were rough
From work on the farm
My hand in hers
All I felt was kindness
Those hands fixed lunch
Butterbeans, corn, and pork chops
So good
Afterwards
She sat in the rocking chair
Lifted me into her lap
My head rested on her chest
Her arms around me
I heard
The soft, steady beat of her heart
Streamed sounds of angels' wings
When they lifted away from Earth
I drifted with them
My eyelids gently closed
Shoulder nestled next to her apron
As I slipped into sleep
Grandma said
There's no better place to dream
Than in the heart of someone who loves you
She was right
I was always in hers
She in mine
A world with kindness
Is where I dream
We will all live
Someday

Notes

"I Remember" and "Dear Rebecca" reference: Vardell Hall was a junior college and preparatory school for girls in Red Springs, North Carolina. It remained active from 1964–1973, located on the site of Flora Macdonald College.

"Church Anniversary" reference: We've always been challenged to live a better life, not in isolation, but with everyone we meet. The poem is about good things achieved when people come together in a shared purpose.

"Gatekeeper" reference: In early childhood years I experienced a recurring dream. Every night I walked past a long line of people, seeing them move through different phases of life—as adults, children, and small twinkles of light. All of them knew me, but I was unsure of how I knew them, though I felt like we were friends. Coming to the end of the line, I climbed on a platform, helped an old man keep a pole gate open so people could walk through. I continually wondered why I was never able to pass through this gate and always had to help the old man with this task. One night I walked through the gate myself. The mystery and meaning will be your interpretation.

Deborah with her grandchildren, Jacob and Skye.

Postscript

We can discard our clothes and shoes, color our hair, cover blemishes, but we cannot hide works of the heart. This is where poetry flourishes. It explains or disdains our emotions, carries us on a sherpa's back to reach the highest peak, glides across each wave, dives and sleeps beside us in the ocean's depth.

Poetry listens as wind moves through a forest, reveals the smallest conversations among trees, birds, and lost travelers. It is the real and imagined journey of souls, from our beginning to ending of time and everything in between. It is the calling that leads us through the wilderness, song of our ancestors, cadence of stories over thousands of years as mankind searches for meaning in our existence. Poetry can be full of surprises, entertains and reveals lives we lead. Like a walk into a shop with shelves stacked with beautiful clothing and things people need, so too can be the world created when poets write their lines. No one is without poetry; only some do not feel it. It's a poet's job to communicate that feeling. Poets enable people to discover the dimensions of who they are.

Poems remain our children. We keep them close to our hearts and nurtured for a time.

Then we have to let them go, print them, and give them a voice. Books may have our names on them, but we have freed the poems within to live another life in the arms of the next reader or listener, to grow and become something wonderful in the mind of another, carrying on the legacy of their heart.

A poet may turn a circumstance into a story that lives forever. When you have a passion to write about life's stepping-stones and showcase intricacies of emotions and relationships, poetry is a great vehicle of transportation. The rhythm, rhyme, syllables, and symbolic images wait for the amalgamation of inspiration, perspiration, and desperation of neurons to fire, and our voices lift up that millisecond phrase, changing a life forever.

I've felt this way since I began writing at five years old. Still a poet in progress, I write because I have to. Memories of favorite poems and classic novels from long ago are reminders and inspiration for me to live a grateful life like my parents did. I hope you find a lyric that lives within your heart here in *One for the Road*. Mine is on every page.

www.ingramcontent.com/pod-product-compliance
Lightning Source LLC
Chambersburg PA
CBHW071008160426
43193CB00012B/1962